The
Language
of Energy

*Accessing, Understanding, and Applying
the Universal Language That Connects
All Beings and All Things*

JASON SHURKA

THE LANGUAGE OF ENERGY: ACCESSING, UNDERSTANDING, AND APPLYING THE UNIVERSAL LANGUAGE THAT CONNECTS ALL BEINGS AND ALL THINGS

DEDICATION

I would like to dedicate this book to the source, which has made it possible to exist in the first place, the Divine universe. Although I physically wrote this book, energetically I did not write anything. This book is merely an expression of the infinite source of Light (energy) that flows through every being and every thing. I am simply a tool that is being used by the Divine universe to express its infinite, eternal, and ever-present flow of Light in a language that everybody can understand, the language of energy, and for that I am grateful.

TABLE OF CONTENTS

ACKNOWLEDGMENTS

First and foremost, I would like to thank the Divine universe for the gifts and blessings that it has provided me with and for the information that it has allowed me to access. Thank you for allowing the ever-present, intelligent, infinite, eternal, and sacred energy of the Divine universe to flow through every thing and every being so effortlessly. Moreover, thank you for giving me the ability to see, feel, and understand this flow of Light in such a way that I can formalize and structure it in order to spread this knowledge, wisdom, and Light to the rest of humanity.

To my beloved parents, thank you for being the greatest support system a soul could ask for. I love you both unconditionally.

To my beautiful sister, whether you know it or not, being around you teaches me an infinitude of lessons. Thank you for always putting up with my deep analysis of your words, and most importantly, thank you for being a medium through which I analyze, feel, and understand the principles that make up the language of energy.

To my dearest soul friend, Talia, thank you for the unconditional Love, guidance, and patience you constantly show me. You are one of the greatest teachers in my life. Our energetic connection has and will only continue to create magic in this world.

To a man I admire greatly, Damien Wynne, thank you for introducing me to the phenomenon of the energetic exchange. You have activated a lot of powerful points that exist in my system of energetic information.

To my soul family, Anton, Michael, Malka, Yaniv, and Liran, thank you for being the unicorns in my life. You have all played a significant role in shaping the way my mind perceives the world around me and the world within me.

I Love you all unconditionally and with absolutely no limitation.

"Everything in the universe is made up of energy vibrating at different frequencies. Each of these frequencies posses a specific vibration, which combine to create your overall vibration of being. All vibrations operate at high and low frequencies, within us and around us."

THE BIG PICTURE

There are healthy people and sick people. There are rich people and poor people. There are happy people and sad people. Growing up, I always wondered why this was the case. Why are there sick people? Why are there poor people? Why are there sad people? When I asked others around me, I always got a similar response. "That's life," I was told. Such a response reflects a direct lack of understanding of the laws that our universe abides by. For years I believed that, and I thought "that's just the way it is," as others would always tell me. The more experience I gained in this world and the more I observed others around me and their behavior, the more I understood that **the differentiation between healthy people and sick people, or rich**

people and poor people, or happy people and sad people is not just a matter of chance, but a matter of choice. We live in an energetic universe in which everything works according to specific laws. Laws that many people are not aware of.

The way energy works in our universe and the laws that our universe abides by are what I like to call "The Language of Energy," as referred to in my other book, *Forming The Formless*. In many ways, *The Language of Energy* is a sequel to *Forming The Formless*. The third chapter of *Forming The Formless* is in fact where I first wrote about the language of energy. In that chapter, I covered foundational ideas and laws, such as the law of vibration, the law of conservation, the law of cause and effect, and the translation of color. The language of energy is of foundational importance if you want to live an exceptional and well directed life, and for that reason, it must be expanded on in order to truly gain what it has to offer. The purpose of this book is to do just that. This is a book for men and women, young and old. The principles contained herein hold the potential to improve your life beyond measure, if used and directed consciously.

Energy is in everything, whether tangible or intangible. Ultimately, energy is the basis of our universe. Attempting to know **what** energy is would be the ego attempting to feel whole and comfortable again. Afterall, **to "know" means to limit all other possibilities.** Energy is limitless, infinite, and formless. It cannot be created or destroyed. It cannot be known; it can only be felt. *The Language of Energy* is not focused on the *what*, but the *how*. Learning the language of energy will teach you how to think in terms of energy, frequency, and vibration, which in turn grants you access to the secrets of the Divine universe, as well as your highest potential at all times in the present moment.

Just look at electricity. Not even the greatest scientists can tell you what it is because it can forever be broken down into smaller and smaller components that will ultimately be deduced to "energy. Although we don't know what electricity truly is, we do know how it works, and by understanding its laws, we have conquered it. Understanding the laws of electricity has led us to be able to create modern day society. By mastering our understanding of its laws, we can light up entire cities with the flip of a single switch. By understanding the laws of electricity, we have taken control of it. Electricity now serves us! For this reason, **understanding the language of energy and learning how to apply its beauty into your daily life through practical application will replace hope and luck with power and direction of the world around you and the world within you.** Understanding the language of energy and applying it into your daily life will allow for your wish to become your command. You can and you will live a life of limitless potential. As a matter of fact, you already are. All you need to do is access it!

The healthy, the rich, and the happy naturally and intuitively follow these universal laws to access the realities that align with their desires in life. They naturally understand and apply the principles that make up the language of energy into their daily lives. Their focus is naturally on what they want instead of what they don't want. On the other hand, the sick, the poor, and the sad simply lack an understanding of the language of energy, and therefore, they live a life that is not aligned with their desires. They tend to focus on what they don't want instead of what they do want. The happy person says, "I want to be happy." The sad person says, "I do not want to be sad." If you pay attention to each phrase, the happy person is focusing on happiness, whereas the sad person is focusing on sadness. Energy does not understand the word "not." **Energy simply hears the subject you are focusing on and manifests**

just that. The subject of the happy person's thought is happiness, whereas the subject of the sad person's thought is sadness. **What you focus on is what will manifest into your life!**

The good news is, learning the language of energy and how to practically apply it into your life is simple! The information contained within this book will teach you the principles that make up the language of energy and how to apply it into your daily life through practical means. I urge you to repeat the applications of the language of energy taught herein until they are engrained into your mind and become a part of you. Once they do, you will naturally and effortlessly lead the life that is aligned with your highest potential at all times.

The purpose of this book is to dissolve the idea that you need to be "lucky" to live a good life and to teach you how to think in a way that will allow you to access any and every reality you so choose. You will no longer be bound to *luck*, as *luck* is a concept that has been created by those who simply lack an understanding of the way the universe works. Luck does not exist. **Luck is simply the effect of a cause. Understanding how to formulate a cause will allow you to effortlessly produce your desired effect.** Using the language of energy to do so will make what we call "luck" no longer an event of chance, but an event of choice!

The language of energy is a beautiful thing. It is important to remember that it is not something that was created, but something that was discovered. It is a foundational universal truth and, therefore, cannot be created. Afterall, **energy cannot be created or destroyed.** Once you gain a grasp of this universal language, you will gain access to your limitless potential, which has always existed and will always exist. Nothing will be out of your reach. Nothing is out of your reach. Your struggles in life will be dissolved, and your desires in life will be at the tip of your fingers waiting for you to choose which reality you would like to manifest in this moment.

My intention is not to influence you, rather to teach you how not to be influenced. My goal is not to tell you what to think, but to teach you how to think, so you can think for yourself. Telling you what to think limits what you can do with the principle of such a thought. Teaching you how to think will effortlessly bring the Divine creator out of you and allow you to express the principles that I am conveying in your own unique and individual way. As you read and digest the following information in this book, make sure that you are aware of my intent. Don't limit yourself to the information that is in this book. Rather, **use the basic principles conveyed herein as foundational tools to further develop your thoughts and how you perceive the world around you and the world within you.**

CHAPTER 1

GAINING ACCESS

"Energy is not created, it is accessed."

Accessing Infinitude

———

Creating your own reality through the use of your thoughts and words is a new age philosophy that is held by many people today. We have been taught that our words and our thoughts create our reality, and most of us genuinely think this is correct. I used to be one of those people. I would practice using conscious thought and conscious speech to create the reality that I wanted to experience. After some thought and quiet contemplation, I understood that I had it all wrong. I questioned what I meant by the word "create," and that is when I understood that I was using the wrong word this entire time to describe what I thought was occurring energetically, when indeed it was something else!

The power of our words and thoughts are beyond our comprehension. The question is, do they really create our reality or do they just access one that has always existed?

All realities exist right here, right now.

Every single possibility.

A happy you.

A sad you.

A married you.

A single you.

A rich you.

A poor you.

A healthy you.

A sick you.

A young you.

An old you.

All of these realities exist, right here, right now.

The Law of Vibration

———

The first thing that must be understood is the Law of Vibration, which I refer to in my book, *Forming The Formless*. The Law of Vibration states that all energy exists in the form of vibrational frequency, and in the energetic world, like attracts like. This means that vibration "x" will only be able to see anything else that is vibrating on vibration "x." Therefore, anything that is emitting vibration "y" or "z" will not be experienced by that which is emitting vibration "x." This is because they exist on different planes.

Everything is vibration. Thought is vibration. Emotion is vibration. Color is vibration. Matter is vibration. What differentiates one form from another is the speed that each form is vibrating at. This vibrational speed is called frequency. Some forms exist at a higher frequency while others exist at a lower frequency, but all forms exist at a specific frequency. **The vibration you emit is the vibration you resonate with. Your vibration is what forms the formless.** In other words, the vibrations you emit will dictate the lens through which you will experience your life. In simple terms, this means that the quality of your thoughts, emotions, words, and feelings (which are all energy, and therefore vibrations) determine not which reality you will create, but which reality you will access! Afterall, reality is energy, and energy cannot be created or destroyed. Therefore, you can never create your own reality, but you can most definitely access that which you desire in the present moment. How? By knowing you already have it. Afterall, **what your mind believes will ultimately be reflected in your physical life.**

What Your Mind Believes, Your Life Reflects

The mind is a beautiful and powerful tool. Many of us let it take over our lives instead of using it to enrich our lives. Many of us allow ourselves to get caught up in our mind. Doing so can make you feel like you are no longer the director of your own life when in fact you are!

Sit back for a moment with your eyes closed and self-reflect on your life. Realize and acknowledge that everything in your life is a direct reflection of your mind. **Everything in your life is a direct reflection of what you choose to focus on.** I am referring to both what you consider as the "good" and the "bad" things.

Your job.

Your health.

Your relationship.

Your financial stability.

Once you understand that everything in your life is a direct reflection of your mind, you will clearly see that you in-fact are the director of your own life. If you happen to be one of the many who sees reflections in your physical life that you are not fond of, it is not because you are not the director, but because you are not familiar with how to direct; you are therefore directing in a way that is working against you! You have likely been focusing on what you don't want instead of what you do want. That's okay! Remember, the purpose of this book is to teach you the language of energy, so you can use it to direct your life in the direction that you desire and access your limitless potential. In other words, the purpose of this book is to teach you how to become the self-serving director of your own life. You can, and you will if you so desire!

What your mind believes and focuses on will always manifest into your life. That means that if you have a problem and constantly focus on that problem instead of the solution, the problem will continue to exist. Alternatively, if you focus on living a life without the problem that you are experiencing, eventually the problem will disappear. Yes, it all begins in the mind! Everything else is just a reflection of it.

The question that remains is, how do you read your mind to become conscious of what and how it thinks in order to know what to change?

Ah, great question! Fortunately, the answer is much simpler than you may think!

Reading your mind and seeing how it works subconsciously has nothing to do with your mind itself, but it has everything to do with the words that come out of your mouth. **You see, your words are a direct reflection of your minds program**, which is comprised of your thoughts and beliefs**. In others words, **your words act as a magnifying glass that give you insights into the current programming of your mind.** As you gain these insights, you will be able to see which part of your minds program is working against you, thus giving you the ability to reprogram your mind in order to improve its reflection that you so deeply cherish—your life!

So, now you are aware of the fact that you must pay attention to your words in order to gain a better understanding of what is going on in your mind. At this point, you might be thinking ,"Great. I see how my mind works now, but that doesn't help me! My mind is my mind. I can't just change my mind. This is how I think!".

Of course you can change you mind! You didn't always think this way; you were taught to think this way from others around you. The good news is, you are not bound to this path of thought for the rest of your life. Simply put, your mind and thought process is a program that you have developed over time. Just like you programmed your mind to think this way, you can reprogram your mind to think in a different way, one that will serve you and bring you closer to your limitless potential.

And of course, the next question is, How? How do you go about changing what and how the mind thinks and believes? How do you reprogram the mind?

Well, the answer lies in the medium that you used to get a better glance of your minds program in the first place. Yes, your words! **You can use your words to reprogram your mind!**

Your words are the keys that you must use to reprogram your mind and thus gain access to infinitude, where all realities exist. Once you understand how to use your words in a beneficial way, all you have to do is reach into the bowl of infinite realities and possibilities and choose that which you would like to experience in this very moment. Your words, which eventually turn into your thoughts and beliefs, act as the hand that reaches into the bowl and chooses the reality it reflects in this very moment. In other words, **your words are the tools that have been provided to you that act as your**

access keys to the infinite realm of possibilities. In this realm, everything is possible.

Adjusting your words to reflect the reality that you want to access and experience will eventually have an impact on your mind. Over time, your mind will actually change its vibration to reflect the reality and vibration you are imprinting onto it through the use of your words.

Remember, your words eventually turn into your thoughts and beliefs, and your thoughts and beliefs are what your mind is comprised of. **Once your mind has been engrained with this new vibration, your physical reality will have no choice but to reflect it. What your mind believes, your life reflects, and this is a law of the universe.** New words become new thoughts. New thoughts become a new mind. A new mind reflects a new life.

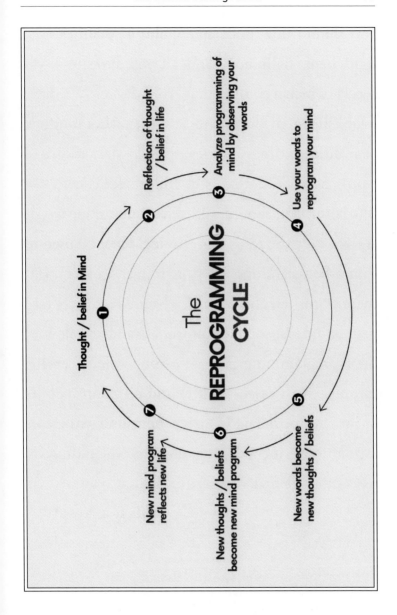

The REPROGRAMMING CYCLE

1. Thought / belief in Mind
2. Reflection of thought / belief in life
3. Analyze programming of mind by observing your words
4. Use your words to reprogram your mind
5. New words become new thoughts / beliefs
6. New thoughts / beliefs become new mind program
7. New mind program reflects new life

You should now understand that all realities exist right here, right now, and all you have to do is access whichever one that you desire. We have established that the key to accessing this infinitude of realities and possibilities exists in your choice of words, something that is in your direct control. At this point, you should understand that these words are not only the tools that can and must be used to gain a better glimpse of your minds program, but these words can and must also be used to reprogram your mind. Now that you understand the flow of the reprogramming cycle, it is time to focus on the formula that can and will teach you the principles of how to formulate your words in order to create a productive mental program that will ultimately reflect the life that you desire.

CHAPTER 2

CHOOSE YOUR WORDS WISELY

"The words you speak, you become."

What you speak, you think. What you think, you access. What you access, you become. What you become, you express. What you express, you experience. What you experience, you are. What you are, you speak. And the cycle continues. Being that we live in an energetic universe, understanding the language of energy will help guide us in formulating and accessing the realities that we would like to experience. If it hasn't been apparent yet, the words you choose to speak are more powerful than you may think. **Thought creates, but words have the power to direct thought and therefore have the power to direct creation.** A direct way to change your thoughts is by changing your words, and changing your words is something you have direct control over. As you already know, to do so you must always speak consciously and listen to the words that are coming out of your mouth. They will provide you with great insights into how your mind works and will therefore allow you to see where the programming of your mind must be improved to reflect a life that is aligned with your desires.

The Power of Speech

The words that come out of your mouth have immense power. **Each word has its own energetic blueprint that resonates with a specific reality.** Never speak a word that you don't want to manifest into your life, not even as a joke. It may sound funny, but this is very important. Once again, **every word has an energetic blueprint, and by speaking a word, you are inheriting its energetic blueprint.** Just like you wouldn't consume poison because it will physically harm you, why would you inherit a poison that will energetically harm you?

Just as the universe has laws, such as the law of oneness, the law of vibration, the law of attraction, the law of conservation, the law of cause and effect, and so on, the universe also has energetic laws that teach us how to use speech as a tool that can help us direct life to go in the direction that we desire.

What are these laws? How do they work?
And why do they work?

Fortunately, these laws are not difficult to learn and understand. They will just take some repetition and practice in order to engrain their use and application into your daily life. I will re-emphasize my intent that I stated in the beginning of this book. **My duty is not to tell you what to think, but to teach you how to think, so you can think for yourself.** I am simply conveying the basic principles of how speech can be used as a tool that can help you direct your life to go in the direction that you desire. My purpose for conveying these principles is because they teach you how to think, without limiting you to what to think. How you use and apply these principles is entirely up to you. The beauty of teaching in this way is that it allows you to apply these universal principles of speech in your own unique and individual way, without imposing the limitations that may exist in my own mind.

The Illusion of Time

First and foremost, to intuitively understand how to formulate your words for your benefit, it is important to understand that time does not exist. **The past does not exist, and neither does the future.** Anything that has ever happened and will ever happen occurred in what we call "the present moment." For the sake of understanding this concept, I want you to think about a major event that happened in what you call your past.

The moment you were born.

When you were born, it happened in what is called "the present," the moment it occurred. Now think about a major event that will happen in what you call your future.

The moment you die.

The moment you die (or *transform*, as I like to call it) also happens in what we call "the present moment," at the moment it occurs. The present moment is where all existence arises from. **The present moment is the only moment that exists.** The present moment is where every single possible reality exists. Most importantly, the **present moment is what you must base your words on in order to allow them to manifest.** So, what words serve you and what words don't?

The Universe Does Not Hear "Not"

Within the language of energy exists a very important law. **The universe does not hear the word "not."** Let's say your goal is to speak in a way that will reflect a life in which you are healthy. To reflect and therefore access such a reality, you may say one of the following:

"I want to be healthy."

or

"I do not want to be sick."

Both have the same intent, but they don't have the same energetic blueprint. The energetic blueprint of your words is what must be paid attention to the most when speaking consciously with the intent of accessing your desired reality. **The energetic blueprint of your speech is always dictated by the subject you are focusing on.** Afterall, the universe only hears the subject you are focusing on, which in turn causes that subject to become part of your reality. In the first example, "I want to be healthy," the subject is being healthy. In the second example, "I do not want to be sick," the subject is being sick. You must always pay attention to the subject of your thoughts. **Focusing on not having something is still focusing on that something,** and always remember that what you focus on is what will manifest into your life.

Remember to always speak consciously, as doing so will cause you to think consciously. As you make the change of transforming your sentences to not include the word "not" and make the center of focus something you do want instead of something you don't want, your life will slowly begin to improve as your physical vibration will reflect greater alignment with your mental vibration. Where and how you choose to focus your energy will dictate the quality of your life. **Focus on negativity, and you access depression. Focus on positivity, and you access happiness. Focus on lack, and you access deficiency. Focus on abundance, and you access prosperity!**

"I WANT" Implies You Don't Already Have

At this point, you understand that the word "not" does not exist in the language of energy and will only take you further out of alignment from the reality you would like to access. Let's take this one step further. **"I want" implies that you don't already have what you are asking for.** Therefore, using the words "I want" before something you would like to access and manifest in the present moment will only cause you to access another reality in which you will attract more *wanting* instead of *having*. Let's use the prior example to see how this works. Let's say that your goal is to speak in a way that will reflect a life in which you are healthy. To reflect and therefore access such a reality, you may say one of the following:

"I want to be healthy."

or

"I will be healthy."

Once again, both have the same intent, but they don't have the same energetic blueprint. Let's start with the fact that they do both share a positive subject, health! This is good; however, the way you are asking to experience health in the first example, "I want to be healthy," implies that you are not already healthy. This implication is the energetic blueprint that you are giving the universe, and therefore, the universe will produce exactly what you asked it for. It will produce more "wanting to be healthy" instead of "being healthy," and in turn, it will not produce the desired outcome that you intended for. **You must always pay attention to the implication you put upon the subject you are focusing on.** Saying "I want" will always attract the experience of more wanting and repel the experience of actually having or experiencing whatever it is that you are focusing on, even if the subject you are focusing on is something positive. Know with all of your soul that you already have everything you want, and you will no longer want it anymore. Why want something if you already have it? Afterall, every reality exists. All you have to do is access it!

"I WILL Is an Illusion"

At this point, you understand that the words "not" and "want" do not exist in the language of energy and will only take you further out of alignment from the reality you would like to access and experience in the present moment.

So, what is the problem with "I will"?

"I will" always keeps your reality in the future, which does not exist. This means, using the words "I will" before something you would like to do or experience will always keep that reality one step ahead of you in the illusory future and never bring it into the present moment, the only moment that truly exists. Let's use the prior example to see how this works. Let's say that your goal is to speak in a way that will reflect a life in which you are healthy. To reflect and therefore access such a reality, you may say one of the following:

"I will be healthy."

or

"I am healthy."

Once again, both have the same intent, but they don't have the same energetic blueprint! It is a much better formulation of words, being that the subject is positive and the implication "will" puts you in closer proximity to accessing the experience of being healthy. However, the last part of the formula that is missing is the **time** in which the reality you are speaking of exists. Because the words "I will" place your reality one step ahead of you in the illusory future, using these words make that entire reality impossible to access and bring into the present moment. So, what is left? How do you formulate your words in such a way that gives you direct access to the reality you are speaking of?

"I AM Is Truth"

So far, we have covered paying attention to **the subject you are focusing on**, **the implication you are setting upon that subject** you are focusing on, and **the time in which the reality you are speaking**

of exists in. So long as you have those three aspects of your speech in line with the reality you would like to access, you are aligned with what I like to call the I-AM formula.

Let's use the prior example to see how this works. Let's say that your goal is to speak in a way that will reflect a life in which you are healthy. To reflect and therefore access such a reality in a way that **focuses on the positive, uses a beneficial implication, and places the reality in present time**, you might say the following:

"I AM HEALTHY!"

Yes! That's it! This sentence follows the I-AM formula and will most definitely put you in direct alignment with what it is that you are speaking of. **I AM is the most powerful pre-phrase to any sentence in the energetic world.** It holds an endless amount of strength and power. More importantly, **the**

principle behind I AM is the final component to the formula since it focuses on placing the reality you are speaking of in the present moment. It is the most effective key that grants you access to the reality that you want to access and experience in the present moment. **I AM gives you direct access to all realities and allows you to experience whatever it is that you are speaking of right here, right now.**

Simplistically, the "I AM" formula is broken down into the following three components, otherwise known as **S.I.P**, that you must always be aware of when speaking of a reality that you intend to manifest:

1. *Subject* of Focus

Example: "I am happy," instead of "I am not sad."

2. *Implication* on Subject

Example: "Thank you for blessing me with health," instead of "Please bless me with health."

3. *Present* Tense

Example: "I am financially stable," instead of "I will be financially stable."

It is important to note that when I refer to an I-AM statement, the only thing that is important is the principle behind it. In other words, the words "I AM" do not have to be a part of it. An I-AM statement is simply a statement that contains the three S.I.P components:

a positive subject, a beneficial implication, and a statement situated in the present moment. For example, "I always figure it out" is considered an I-AM statement because it focuses on the positive, implies you already have what you need, and is stated in the ever-present moment. So long as you consciously include S.I.P into your daily speech, you are following the I-AM formula and will therefore be aligned with accessing the reality you desire and bringing it into your present moment.

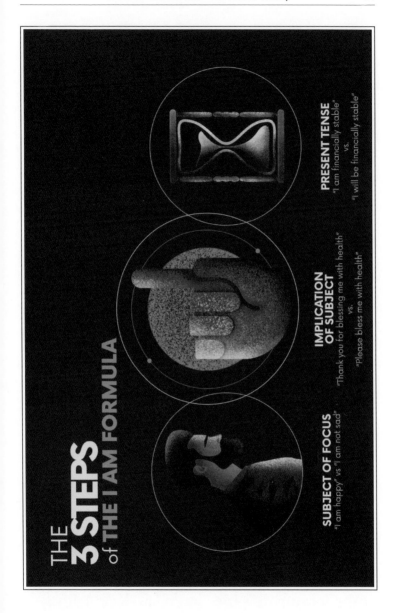

Accessing "I AM" Instantaneously

———

You now understand and know how to practically apply the I-AM formula into your daily life. Sure, it will take some practice, but I promise that you will get used to it! Once you do, you will surely experience the magic of it until it becomes another standard in your ever-evolving path of life. So, what causes one I-AM statement to be accessed quicker than another? If the

I-AM formula is so flawless, why doesn't it manifest the second it is spoken or written? Is it even possible for an I-AM statement to be accessed the second it is spoken or written?

These are all great questions! Of course you can access the reality of which you speak of instantaneously, but you will have to add some extra components to the formula in order to do so. Although using the I-AM formula to base your statements in the present is an extremely effective key, it is not the final key to the formula of accessing your desired reality and bringing it into the present moment instantaneously. Once you practice applying the I AM formula into your daily life, the next thing you must learn to apply is how to manifest your statement instantaneously, without having to wait a prolonged period of time between your I AM statement and actually accessing the reality you are speaking of by bringing it into the present moment right here, right now. The next and final steps following your successful application of the I AM formula is what I like to call **I.B.V.:** Intent. Belief. Visualization.

The Final Steps

It all starts with **intent**. Your intent is reflected by the words that you speak. Intent is directive. Intent is what steers your reality into one direction or another. However, **intent is not everything.** For example, if your intent is to be healthy but the words that you speak are, "I am not sick," you are speaking in such a way that will cause the language of energy to work against you. **If you have an intention but don't follow the language of energy to speak of it, you are inherently setting your intention up for failure and steering yourself in a direction that you did not intend.**

The next step is **belief.** Belief is one of the most important steps in the process. Without it, no matter how much you speak of a reality, that reality will never be able to be accessed in the present moment. Belief creates the possibility for something to be real in the first place. **The only thing creating a gap between the moment you speak of your I-AM statement and the moment you access the reality of that I-AM statement is your belief.** If you believe something to be impossible, you inherently block yourself from the possibility from the start. If you believe something to be possible, you will always find a way. If you believe something to be difficult, you also believe that it will take you longer to access that reality. However, if you believe something to be easy, accessing that reality will be a breeze for you. **Remember, your life is a direct reflection of what you believe is possible.** The more difficult you believe the reality of which you are speaking of to be attained, the longer it will take you to access it and bring it into the present moment for you to experience it.

Let me give you a scenario for you to better understand. Let's say you set an intention with an aligned I-AM statement to win the lottery this week, and you also set an intention with an aligned I-AM statement to go to the movies this week. You probably **believe** that winning the lottery this week is a reality that is more difficult to achieve and access than going to the movies this week, and therefore, your belief in each will determine how long it will take for each reality to be accessed in the present moment. Although your intention was set correctly, your belief was not, and you will therefore experience a major gap between your I-AM statement and actually accessing the reality, which reflects that statement in the present moment, if you ever access it at all. This is because your life is a direct reflection of your mind, and your mind is comprised of your beliefs and thoughts. You now know that all realities exist right here, right now. With this knowledge, both realities are equally accessible! Your belief is the only thing getting in your way. Afterall, **the only limits that exist are the ones that you believe, and therefore set for yourself.**

The final step to access the reality that reflects your aligned I-AM statement instantaneously is **visualization.**

Visualization is manifestation.
Visualization is imagination.
Visualization is realization.
Visualization is creation.

Visualization is simply manifestation in progress. It is one of the most powerful tools at your disposal to access and experience any and every reality in the present moment. **Visualization is a tool that gives you the ability to literally carve out the energetic blueprint that you would like to access and manifest right here, right now.** If you can visualize it, you can manifest it. **Visualization is also an effective tool in believing what it is that you are conveying through your I-AM statement.** The clearer your visualization of the reality that reflects your statement, the easier it will be to believe. Of course, the clearer your visualization, the more energy you are allocating towards accessing that reality of which you are visualizing into your present moment. The more energy you allocate to visualizing the reality that you would like to access, the more energy you are giving it to come forth. **Afterall, energy flows where attention goes.**

It is important to remember that the universal law of balance makes visualization a double-edged sword.

Although it is a tool that can be used to serve you, it is also a tool that can be used to harm you if not used correctly. By visualizing what you don't want, you bring yourself closer to that reality. Visualization can also be used as a tool to see what reality you are in resonance with. In other words, if it is easier for you to visualize something you don't want instead of something you do; this is a clear indicator that you must focus on speaking consciously in order to change that visualization before you access a reality you don't want in your present moment.

Your intent must be expressed in alignment with the I-AM formula; your belief must be undoubted, and your visualization must be clear. Visualization seeded with intention and belief is extremely powerful. The stronger your belief, the shorter the gap will be between expression and accession. Visualization will enhance the strength of your belief. It is your secret weapon.

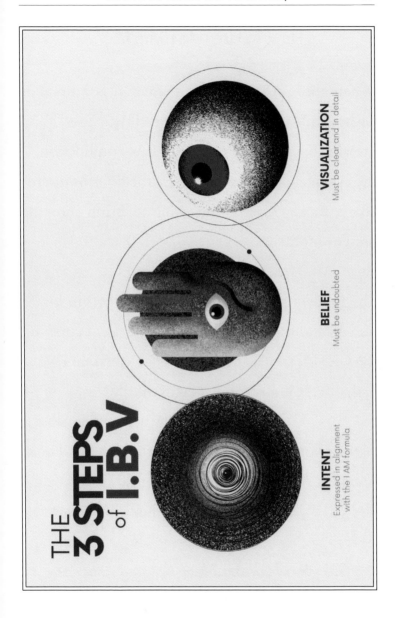

THE
3 STEPS of I.B.V

INTENT
Expressed in alignment
with the I AM formula

BELIEF
Must be undoubted

VISUALIZATION
Must be clear and in detail

How To Use I-AM with I.B.V.

———

When the I-AM formula is used in conjunction with I.B.V, nothing is impossible. You quite literally become unstoppable. This conjunction is the complete key that will open the door of instant access to any reality you want to bring into the present moment.

The following is a personal story for you to better understand the true power and strength of applying the I-AM formula and I.B.V in conjunction to your daily life. It is absolutely magnificent!

I set my original intention to write my first book, *Forming The Formless*, in April of 2017. On April 17th 2017, I wrote the following entry in my journal:

> *"The idea of writing a book has been circulating in my mind. I know I am not ready yet but one day I will be. Whether that day is in 5 years or*

20 years from now, I am in no rush. When I gain enough experience, I will effortlessly write my first book. I look forward to whenever that may be!"

Pay attention to the words I wrote, and you will see the thoughts and beliefs I had in my mind were acting as my limitations. I set my **intent**, but the words I used did not follow the

I-AM formula as they kept the reality of me writing the book way ahead of me in the illusory future. On top of that, I didn't **believe** that I was ready, and I most definitely could not **visualize** the book anytime in my near future.

On July 2nd 2018, I wrote the following entry in my journal:

"I am very inclined to write a book. I have been for the past year now. I know I am still

considered young and that I am not ready. With that being said, I also know that I have what it takes to write a book that will spread Light on this earth. I've had ideas but have not come down to how I want to formulate it and what I would like to include in it. Universe, please provide me with the energy, time, and power to write a book filled with Light and wisdom in the near future".

Once again, my words reflect that my thoughts were still limiting me, only this time my limitations decreased. Instead of placing the reality "5 years or 20 years from now," I placed it in the "near future." Not perfect, but most definitely in closer proximity to the present moment. My **intent** to write the book existed, but I was still not in alignment with the I-AM formula as my words still placed the reality in the illusory future. My **belief** was stronger, but the fact that I still believed I was "too young" and "not ready" caused my belief to not be strong enough to bring that reality into the present moment, and therefore, my belief limited me. My **visualization** was still not clear, thus accessing the reality was still not a possibility.

On April 9th 2019, I wrote the following entry in my journal:

"I've decided. I am going to write a book! For about two years now, I've been thinking about this and trying to visualize it. I've constantly felt that I was not ready, but today… I AM READY! I see the book in my mind's eye. It's going to be a foundational book. Its purpose is to improve one's methods of visualizing and understanding the world. I am going to put together a table of contents tonight with a basic outline. From there, I am going to write the introduction to help me visualize the book

*accordingly and put me on the right path. I see
this book reaching the masses. My intentions of
writing it is to jump-start my purpose in life
and begin the change that this world deserves.
I am ready. I am calm. I am grounded. I am
excited to experience this journey! May this be
the start of a beautiful part of my life."*

This time, my **intent** aligned with the I-AM formula, my **belief** of being able and ready was undoubted, and I could clearly **visualize** the entire book in my minds eye from beginning to end. I began the book that same day. Two months following this journal entry, the book was completed, accepted by a publisher, and is now available in all marketplaces including Amazon, Google books, Apple books, and Barnes & Noble.

This book, on the other hand, was a whole different story. This is because I understood how to use the language of energy to help serve me. I set my original intention to write this book, *The Language of Energy*, in February of 2020.

On February 14th 2020, I wrote the following entry in my journal:

> *"I have officially decided that I am going to write a second book. I see this book being revolved around teaching others how to use their words to achieve their wildest dreams, to access the infinite present moment… where all existence arises from. I am ready."*

My **intent** was set in alignment with the I-AM formula, my **belief** was undoubted and my **visualization** was clear enough to see what the purpose and intention of the book was going to be. I began the book that same moment. Today, as I am writing this very paragraph, it is February

17th, 2020. Three days have passed since I decided that I am going to write my second book and I have already completed the table of contents, the acknowledgments, the dedication, the introduction, chapter one and half of chapter two. My **intention** is aligned, my **belief** is undoubted, and I can **visualize** how the rest of the book is going to be formulated in detail. As a matter of fact, I sketched my visualization onto a piece of paper before starting to write it in the form of an in-depth table of contents that the universe allowed me to access instantaneously, being that my **intent**, **belief**, and **visualization** were all clear and aligned with the present moment.

This is what the beauty of understanding and applying the I-AM formula in conjunction with I.B.V can and will do to your life! This is the beauty of the language of energy.

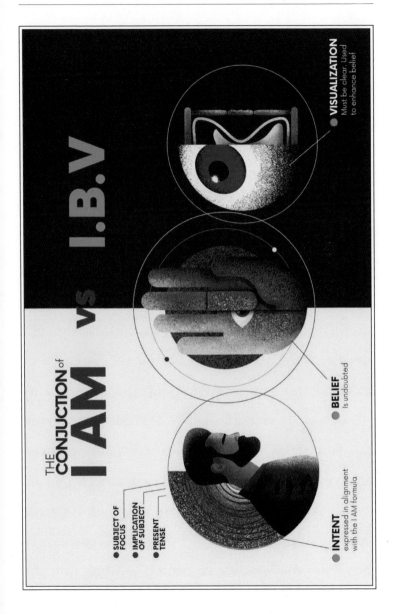

The Denial Controversy

The I-AM formula in conjunction with I.B.V can be used in so many ways, such as physical healing and emotional healing. The applications are endless! If you are sick, you can say or write "I am healthy." If you are sad, you can say or write "Thank you for blessing me with unconditional joy." If you are experiencing financial lack, you can say or write "Thank you for granting me financial stability and success." At this point in my thought process, when I was first learning the language of energy, I thought to myself, "Wait a second! Isn't this denial? If you are sick, you are sick. If you are sad, you are sad. If you are experiencing financial lack, you most definitely are NOT financially stable and successful! Why would you deny the apparent facts? Wouldn't denial just bring you further from the reality that you are intending to bring into the present moment?"

The answer is quite simple actually. Denial does just that. **Denial brings you further from the reality that you are intending to bring into the present moment.** The only thing is… this is not denial! On the contrary, you must always acknowledge and accept your reality before accessing a new one. Why? Because if you resist your reality, you only strengthen its presence. **What you resist, persists.** However, **the second you accept your reality is the second you will be granted the ability to transform it.** Once you have entered a state of pure acknowledgment and acceptance of your current circumstance at hand and have dissolved all resistance to it, you will be able to use the I-AM formula in conjunction with I.B.V to access a new reality and bring it into the present moment instantaneously. This can only be done when coming out of a pure place of acceptance. Coming out of a poisonous place of resistance will deem your I-AM statement invalid, as resistance does not allow energy to flow in the first place. Therefore, it will not allow you to bring the reality that you are speaking of into the present moment. **Resistance closes the doors of the universe when it comes to the language of energy. Acceptance keeps them wide open, allowing the universe to hear you and provide as soon as you allow it to.**

My next thought was, "Okay, but even if I have acknowledged and accepted my reality of being sick, speaking or writing 'I AM HEALTHY' is still a direct contradiction of my current reality. Why would contradicting my current reality of being sick help me bring the new reality of being healthy into the present moment?"

Another great question!

Remember, all realities exist right here, right now. Therefore, all realities are your current realities, not just the one you are experiencing. In other words, right here, right now, exists a reality where you are sick while a different reality simultaneously exists in which you are healthy. Just because you are currently in alignment with the reality in which you are sick does not mean the reality in which you are healthy does not exist in this very moment. The only reason you are not experiencing the reality in which you are healthy is because you are not in resonance with it. So if you are sick, speaking or writing a statement aligned with the I-AM formula, such as "I am healthy," or "Thank you for blessing me with health" in conjunction with I.B.V is simply assisting you in adjusting your frequency to resonate with the reality in which you are healthy. This will allow you to attract and access the physical experience of being healthy that exists right now into the present moment. **Your I-AM statement is not a denial of the current reality you are experiencing, but rather it is inviting forth the reality you would like to bring into the present moment.** Not only will practicing this consciously aligned form of speech help you energetically, physically, and spiritually, but it will also help you effortlessly change your physical actions and behaviors to enable you to successfully access the reality that you are speaking of with your aligned I-AM statement in conjunction with I.B.V.

How This Works Energetically

How would speaking or writing "I am healthy" or "Thank you for blessing me with health" rid you of your sickness. How would speaking or writing "Thank you for blessing me with unconditional joy" rid you of your sadness? How would speaking or writing "Thank you for granting me financial stability and success" rid you of financial lack? Understanding just how this works will allow you to replace hope and luck with power and direction of the world around you and the world within you. It all starts with the law of vibration. As you already know, the law of vibration states that all energy exists in the form of vibrational frequency and in the energetic world like attracts like. Simplistically, the law of vibration implies that the **vibration you emit is the vibration you resonate with,** which will in turn dictate the lens which you experience your life through. The following is an excerpt from *Forming The Formless* in the form of an analogy that may help you understand this idea better:

"Do you ever listen to the radio? Whether you listen to AM or FM, have you ever asked yourself what that 'AM' and 'FM' is? The radio works on vibrational frequency. The difference between AM and FM is simply how the vibration is being modulated. Regardless, both AM and FM radio work through different vibrations which means they both work by the same principles and laws. The law of vibration. If you want to listen to the news, you might tune to a specific AM channel whether it be 1010AM or 770AM. If you want to listen to music, you might tune to a specific FM channel whether it be 104.3FM or 97.1FM. You get

the idea. The point is that each channel chooses a vibration on which to host their radio shows. By tuning to that vibration, you have gained access to the show and can therefore either listen to the news or sing along to the music. These basic principles of how vibration works apply to all vibrations in the universe. This includes words, thoughts, and beliefs. Health and sickness are vibrations. Happiness and sadness are vibrations. Abundance and lack are vibrations. You can look at these vibrations (realities) as channels that exist just like 1010AM or 97.1FM. **Your mind is the tuner that chooses what vibration (reality) it would like to tune to through the medium of your words, thoughts, and beliefs.** *If you program your mind to think thoughts of health through your words, you are tuning to the radio station of health and therefore experience your life through that lens. However, if you program* *your mind to think thoughts of sickness through your words, you will experience your life through the lens of sickness and therefore perceive the world around you accordingly. It is important to remember the following: although there may be many different radio stations, they all exist simultaneously and in parallel to one another. In other words, let's say there are ten different radio stations for you to be able to tune into. There is a different song or talk show being hosted on each of the ten channels. If you happen to be on channel four, you will simply hear what is on channel four. This also means that when you are tuned into channel four, you are not able to hear what is happening on channel one, two, three, five, six, seven, eight, nine, or ten. Although you cannot hear what is being hosted on the other channels, you know that they exist simultaneously with channel four. They are all equally accessible. A channel represents a reality. All realities exist right here, right now. Most importantly, all realities are equally accessible, energetically. You are in complete control of what channel you would like to tune into. You are the director. Now that you are aware of the power of your mind, speak consciously, think consciously, and tune away."*

Your experience of life is simply based on which reality you are energetically tuned into. The reality that you experience in the present moment is a direct reflection of the vibrational frequency of your mind, which is made up of your thoughts and beliefs and directed by your words. Every word, every thought, and every belief exist at a specific vibration, and that vibration dictates what you can and can't access in the present moment. Here is an example to help you better understand what is truly being said here, so you can practically apply it to your daily life.

Let's say you are experiencing financial lack. This reality is correlated to certain thoughts and beliefs that are reflected through your words. For example:

"Why am I so terrible at saving and managing my money?"

or

"I won't be able to afford my rent in 3 months"

or

"I can never pay my credit card bill on time."

If you pay attention to these thoughts, they all exist on the same vibration that financial lack exists on. In other words, your words, thoughts, and beliefs are only going to make you experience more financial lack since you are focused on the lack instead of the gain (lessons) that the experience of lack can teach you. Since all of these words, thoughts, and beliefs exist on the same vibration (reality) as financial lack, what you are in-fact doing by speaking these words and thinking these thoughts is staying in tune with the vibration (reality) of lack. Therefore, you will continue experiencing this reality that you do not want to experience. Afterall, the vibration you tune to through your words and your thoughts dictates the reality that you will experience your life through in the present moment. So, at this point it is safe to say that if you want to change your reality, you must first change your vibration. To change your vibration, you must change the things that are emitting those vibrations in the first place: **Your words!**

Once you completely understand how all of this works energetically through the law of vibration, you can consciously and freely use speech to tune to whatever vibration (reality) it is that you would like to experience in the present moment. The beautiful thing is, once you tune to a different frequency, your physical actions and behaviors will change too! For example, let's say you are someone who has a problem with over-eating or you constantly eat foods that are not beneficial to you out of an irresistible habit. If and when you begin to speak and think consciously with the intent of tuning out of that vibration and into a healthier vibration, you will naturally start to see a decline in your physical desire to over eat along with a decline in the physical desire to consume the unhealthy foods you used to love so much! To shift from the unhealthy vibration into the healthy vibration, you must allow the healthy vibration to become a part of your conscious and subconscious mind.

"I eat only what is necessary, and I consume only the foods that manifest health. I am a healthy eater".

Don't be afraid to speak these words over and over again until they are a part of you. Feel free to write them every morning before you start your day. You can even put them up on a wall that you pass by every morning in your home. Once these vibrations become engrained into your mind, your physical body, your actions, and your behavior will have no choice but to change their course in order to reflect the vibration that your mind is emitting! **Remember, to attain something, you must first tune to its vibrational frequency.** In order to tune to its vibrational frequency, you must do so through the use of your words, which eventually turn into your thoughts and beliefs, which is what your mind is comprised of, which is ultimately the reflection of your life! The power is yours, and you have been provided with the necessary tools to claim it! The last tool you have yet to discover is silence.

The Power of Silence

Silence is an extremely powerful tool that can be used to increase the strength and power of your expressed words. Energetically, silence is used to harvest potential energy (energy being stored up) in order to create a powerful form of kinetic energy

(energy being released). **Potential energy is the equivalent of unexpressed or unreleased energy, such as thoughts** that exist in the mind. **Kinetic energy is the equivalent of expressed and released energy, such as words,** which are the physical manifestations of your thought. Think of it like shooting a pebble out of a sling shot. The further you pull back the pebble, the further the pebble will go. This is because energetically pulling back the pebble builds up potential energy, which is then released in the form of kinetic energy. **Of course, the more potential energy you harvest, the more kinetic energy can be released.** This is exactly how silence works. Your state of silence is the equivalent of pulling the pebble back in the slingshot right before you launch it. **Silence harvests potential energy while verbal expression is the release of that potential energy in the form of kinetic energy.** The more you practice silence, the more potential energy you will build up, which will cause your words (the release of kinetic energy) to be extremely powerful when you do decide to express them. Speak only when necessary.

Hopefully, you now understand why choosing your words wisely is so important. Speech is a tool that is in your direct control. It is a tool that gives you the ability to carve out the energetic blueprint that you would like to access and manifest right here, right now. It is a tool that allows you to claim the power that was given to you. You have been given the appropriate tools to practice conscious and aligned speech, which will naturally turn into conscious and aligned thought, which will then be reflected in your life. You have been taught the following principles regarding speech:

The universe does not hear the word "not."
"I want" implies you don't already have.
"I will" is an illusion.
"I am" is the key.

You have been taught the I-AM formula, otherwise known as S.I.P, which is broken down into the following three components that you must always be aware of when speaking of a reality that you intend to manifest:

Subject of Focus

Implication on Subject

Present Tense

It may take some practice in the beginning, but with practice comes perfection, and in this case, with perfection comes a life you've always dreamed of. Once you understand that time is an illusion and all existence arises out of the present moment, you will naturally and intuitively be able to place your statements in the present moment quite effortlessly in order to access your desired reality by bringing it into your present moment. Once you add I.B.V, which is **intent**, **belief**, and **visualization** to the I-AM formula, you become unstoppable and are able to access the reflection of your I-AM statement instantaneously. Remember, **your intent must be in alignment with the I-AM formula**, your **belief must be undoubted**, and **your visualization must be clear,** which will enhance your belief. Start small, and ease your way up the ladder. Begin by setting your intention to access a reality in the present moment that you wholeheartedly know and truly believe with no doubt whatsoever, a reality you can fully visualize in detail. As you gain more confidence in yourself and in your ability to believe, you will be able to access a wider range of realities in a much shorter period of time. You will see that the limitations of your beliefs will start to dissolve. There is no limit to what you can achieve, and when the limitations of your beliefs are stripped away, you will experience this first hand!

Always keep in mind that verbalizing an I-AM statement that is in contradiction with your current reality is not denial, but merely an inviting-forth of the reality you would like to bring into the present moment. **Only once you accept your current reality can you transform it and access a new reality.**

You have been taught the principles behind the law of vibration and how to directly apply that law with straight forward formulas into your daily life through the use of speech. Although conscious speech will bring you a long way, there are still other factors that play a major role in your understanding and application of the language of energy. Once these other factors are digested and understood, the universe will naturally grant you full access to your highest potential at all times in the present moment. So far, you have learned how to use internal tools, such as conscious speech, according to the law of vibration to access the realm of infinite realities and bring the reality which you so choose into your present moment. In addition to internal tools, the universe has also provided us with external tools, but these may only be used once a true understanding of how the language of energy works with our external environment is attained wholly and fully.

CHAPTER 3

THE ENERGETIC EXCHANGE

"The energetic exchange is the inevitable interaction of energetic information between any and every form of energy. Any experience between two energetic forms, no matter how brief or prolonged, results in an energetic exchange of information between those forms of energy and is imprinted into the energetic universe for eternity."

Once you understand the principles that make up the language of energy, you can apply those principles to learning how to use your external environment and surroundings as a tool to access the realm of infinite realities and bring the reality which you so choose into your present moment. Once you do, you will ultimately replace hope and luck with power, and you will begin to direct the world around you and the world within you. The law of vibration plays a major role in understanding how to apply the principles that make up the language of energy in a way that serves you. If you are finding it too difficult to be aware and conscious of your speech in order to gain a greater insight of the programming of your mind, fortunately for you, there is another way! Some say this way is easier than having to speak and think consciously. I will leave that up to you to decide.

Just as your words and thoughts are energy in the form of different vibrations, your external environment is no different. When I refer to your "external environment" and "surroundings," I am referring to things, such as the people you spend your time with, the relationships you attract, your behavior and actions, and even the hardships you are experiencing in your life. They are all ultimately reflections of the vibration you are resonating with. They are all direct reflections of the programming of your mind. **Your external environment is the vibratory result of the vibration that the program of your mind currently operates at.**

Just like words act as a magnifying glass to seeing what is going on in your mind, your external environment can be used in just the same way! This is because both your words and your external environment are direct reflections of your mind and can thus be used to gain a deeper understanding of your mind as a whole. **Not only does your external environment act as a tool to look deeper into the programming of your mind, but it also acts as a**

tool to reprogram your mind. Therefore, a simple conscious change in your external reality will reflect a change in your internal reality.

Some may say you are the product of your environment. This is true, and so is the direct opposite! Your environment is a direct product of you. This is the beauty of the language of energy. **It teaches one to think in a reflective way, which only provides one with more resources to replace chance with choice.** The beauty of the balance in the language of energy is that you never have to focus on both the internal and the external simultaneously since they are simply reflections of one another. If you are having trouble changing something in your internal reality, simply change its reflection in your external reality, and your internal reality will follow. The opposite is also true. If you are having trouble changing something in your external reality, simply change its reflection in your internal reality, and your external reality will follow. For example, if you happen to be a very messy and unorganized person and don't know how to change that external reality, simply start eating cleaner and healthier. The cleaner you are internally, the cleaner you will naturally and effortlessly want to be externally. Alternatively, if you happen to be a very unhealthy person and don't know how to change that internal reality, simply start keeping your external reality cleaner and more organized. The cleaner you keep your external environment, such as your home or your work place, the cleaner you will naturally and effortlessly want to be internally.

Everything is an Exchange

The universe is one infinite ball of energetic information. Whether tangible or intangible, everything is made up of energy. Being that we are both tangible beings (the body) and intangible beings (the soul), we all hold immense amount of energetic information and subconscious memory that is ever-present and not bound to the illusion of the linear passage of time that we experience in our physical lives. As a matter of fact, **all we really are is energetic information.** Just as we are made up of energetic information, so is everything else in the world: not every being, but every thing. Yes, this includes tangible and intangible forms beyond just humans, such as animals, plants, trees, rocks, water, words, emotions, thoughts, beliefs, and everything else in the universe. All forms of energy interact with one another through the language of energy, through what I like to call *"the energetic exchange."*

So, what is an energetic exchange? **An energetic exchange is the inevitable interaction of energetic information between any and every form of energy. Any experience between two energetic forms, no matter how brief or prolonged, results in an energetic exchange between those forms of energy and is imprinted into the energetic universe for eternity.** Direct and relatable forms of an energetic exchange between human beings could be a conversation, a simple hug, or even just being in the presence of one another (even if no conversation occurs). Fortunately, the energetic exchange and its practical uses go much further than just a conversation or a hug. The more conscious you are of the energetic exchange, the more information you will be able to access from the infinite field of energetic information that is ever-present throughout the entire universe.

In order to be able to use an energetic exchange to your benefit, you must first be aware that the phenomenon exists, as well as understand the basics of how it works in principle. The energetic exchange extends beyond just human beings. For example, consider the Great Pyramid of Giza in Egypt. First, you must understand that although the Great Pyramid of Giza is a physical and tangible structure, it also holds an immense amount of energetic information. This energetic information consists of its construction, the beings that constructed it, all the periods of time it experienced throughout history, and everything that has ever happened in those time periods up until present day. If only the Great Pyramid of Giza could talk, imagine how many mysteries would be solved! Well, the Great Pyramid of Giza CAN talk, and understanding and applying the principles behind the energetic exchange may grant you the ability to listen to its story! Ultimately, the Great Pyramid of Giza holds all the answers we are looking for in the form of energetic information. Since it experienced the answers to all the unanswered and unsolved mysteries we are trying to comprehend, those answers are also a part of the Pyramid's energetic information, and we therefore have access to it through its field of energetic information. Tapping into this field of energetic information would give us access to the answers of the questions our world has been asking for centuries. How were the pyramids built? Who built them, and what was their purpose? Please be aware that I brought up the example of the Great Pyramid of Giza simply to make you aware of the limitless potential of the energetic exchange. I, personally, do not know how to tap into such depths of the energetic field just yet; however, it is most definitely a possibility, and there are people in this world that can do it.

Energetically, the Great Pyramid of Giza and a human being have something in common; they are both made up of energetic information. This means that in our souls exists all the information of any and all energetic exchanges that we have ever and will ever experience. Remember, time does not exist in the energetic world. Every reincarnation that your soul has experienced is stored into your soul's energetic DNA. The more tapped in you are to yourself spiritually, the more information you can access on the level of your soul from all energetic experiences your soul has ever and will ever experience. The point here is that even by simply being in the presence of someone or something, you are naturally indulging in an energetic exchange between you and the other being or thing.

The following is an entry from my journal that I wrote on February 26th, 2020 regarding a personal experience that I had that emphasizes the importance of the energetic exchange and what can be achieved through it:

"I've been staying at this very remote village in the Guanacaste province of Costa Rica for the past few days. This village is absolutely incredible. At first when I arrived, I was extremely uncomfortable due to the primitive nature of all the people here. Shoes are not something normal over here which blew my mind because it is in the middle of the jungle. Everyone is barefoot! I also realized that when they eat, utensils are never used. Yes, they eat with their hands I was in complete awe for my first couple of days here.

These people walk barefoot, they eat simple food and all of it is done with their hands yet they are so happy and connected spiritually. After a few days of wondering what was going on, I decided to put myself in their shoes (not literally, because they wear no shoes) and started walking barefoot and eating with my hands. After just a few hours of indulging in what I thought were primitive actions and behaviors, it dawned on me. I immediately understood that they are not the primitive ones... I am! Walking barefoot created this energetic connection between me and the earth. It also forced me into pure presence since I had to pay attention to every step I took. This state of presence allowed me to gain insights I have never pondered before due to the energetic exchange of information that was occurring between me and the earth below me. I noticed the same thing with food. Eating with my hands allowed me to connect to my food in a way I never thought was possible. I gained a higher level of awareness regarding the right pace to eat at in order for my body to digest the food in a healthy way. I also immediately felt what was good for my body to eat and what wasn't. For example, I am sensitive to gluten. After a couple of days of becoming more in tune with my food, just holding a piece of bread that contained gluten immediately made me feel uncomfortable and nauseous before it ever even entered my body! Thank you, intuition, for guiding me so effortlessly and giving me the ability to access such holistic and sacred information about the world around me and the world within me. With infinite Love, Jason."

Those who are considered in modern day as "primitive" are spiritually and energetically advanced; whereas, those who are considered in modern day as "advanced" are spiritually and energetically primitive. Although modern inventions and technology have allowed us to progress in many ways, they have also caused a great energetic disconnect between us and the world around us, as well as the world within us. **Modern inventions and technology have made the need for the presence and awareness of the energetic connection obsolete. What we call man-kind's progression has actually blocked the possibility for energetic exchanges to occur in many ways and has made us sick, thus contributing to the demise of humanity's health.** Shoes block the energetic exchange between us and the earth. We live in cement caves that we call our homes, and we sleep on mattresses instead of sleeping on the ground. We are energetic beings, and the earth is energetically charged. By walking barefoot and being in constant contact with the ground below us (earth), an energetic exchange occurs, which rejuvenates our entire being. However, we have lost our ground; therefore, we are no longer grounded.

Eating utensils block the energetic exchange between us and our food. We have been domesticated by society to feel that being barefoot and eating with your hands is improper and primitive. Due to the blockage of these energetic exchanges, we have become numb to the vibrations around us and within us and, therefore, have allowed ourselves to unknowingly create hell on earth. This is simply the physical reflection of the energetic blockages that exists throughout modern society due to the decline of energetic exchanges occurring between us and the natural world.

However, I am not suggesting to walk around New York City barefoot or eat with your hands in an upscale restaurant. **To resist the collective vibration of your surroundings in a way that upsets others will create an energetic blockage in and of itself.** I am merely suggesting to indulge in these activities where the collective vibration is in alignment with such actions, in order to allow these beneficial energetic exchanges to occur or permit yourself to respectfully indulge in these activities without upsetting those around you in any way. In other words, don't be afraid to walk barefoot in nature to energetically connect to the earth below you and embrace eating with your hands in places like your home or wherever else is acceptable without resisting your surroundings in order to energetically connect to your food.

The energetic exchange is limitless in its nature. Although an energetic exchange can be beneficial, it can also be harmful depending on who or what you are indulging in the energetic exchange with. For this reason, who you choose to surround yourself with is more important than one may think. Every interaction you have with another soul is an exchange of energetic information, and that exchange works both ways. Information from your soul is given to the other's soul, and information from the other's soul is given to you. This is the balance of the universe. This is the energetic exchange.

Be Conscious of Your External Reality

Although your external environment, such as your friends, your relationships, and your behavior and actions, has the power to keep you in a repetitive cycle of dissatisfaction, the balance of the universe gives your external environment the power to take you out of that repetitive cycle of dissatisfaction and lead a life filled with Light, Peace, and Love. Your external reality has a major effect on you, and observing it can and will most definitely be extremely beneficial, so long as you know how to look at it through a lens that will allow you to learn more about the programming of your mind. **Your external reality is merely a reflection of your mind, and your mind is merely a reflection of your external reality.** Observing your external reality is just as powerful as observing your words when it comes to understanding the program of your mind. **Just like your words, observing your external reality is not only used to gain insights into the programming of your mind, but it can also be used to reprogram your mind in order to reflect the reality that you would like to tune into in the present moment.** The more conscious you are of your surroundings, the more you will feel, understand, and know how to use the energy around you and within you as a tool to serve you in life.

Using Your External Reality as a Tool

The physical poisons we consume are direct reflections of the vibration that our minds are operating at. Drinking. Smoking. Eating unhealthy food. **All of these actions of consuming physical poisons act as a great indicator of the vibration that your mind is operating at.** The only reason these physical poisons are desirable to you and make you feel "high" when you ingest them is because your vibration is currently lower than the vibration of these poisons, and when you ingest them, the higher vibration of the poison relative to the lower vibration you currently possess gives you a feeling of being "high." Eventually, when you raise your vibration above that of these poisons, you will no longer desire them since ingesting them will no longer make you feel high. Once you raise your vibration above that of these poisons, ingesting them will actually make you feel sick since their vibration is lower relative to your new and higher vibration. In other words, ingesting them will take you down instead of bringing you up. Once that happens, you know you have succeeded in raising your vibration. **So, the key is not to resist these poisons, but to vibrationally rise above them**. Doing so will inevitably dissolve your craving for them from your system, thus allowing you to continue on your path of elevation throughout your life. Once again, it is important to remember that the law of balance in the universe makes these poisons both something useful and harmful in your life, depending on how you choose to use them. You can either use these poisons to bring you down by ingesting them or lift you up by using them as vibratory indicators.

Once you understand that all you have to do is raise your vibration relative to the poisons in your external reality in order to dissolve them from your reality, the next question is:

"How do you raise your vibration?"

That's a great question! There are many ways to raise your vibration of being; however, in order to keep this information simple and digestible, I am going to break down how to do so into two main parts. **The first way to raise your vibration is by using your actions and objects in your external environment as a tool. The second way is by using the people in your external environment as a tool.**

In regard to using your actions and objects in your external environment as a tool to raise your vibration, **the first step is achieved by focusing on the physical place that you spend the most time in, which is what I like to call your "zone."** For some of you, this may be your home, and for others this place may be your bedroom or your office. Whichever it is, **your zone is what has the biggest impact on you as it is the closest physical reflection of you that exists.** This impact can be used to either serve you or to harm you. You are in direct and complete control of what is allowed into your zone and what is not allowed into your zone. Begin by observing your zone and everything that exists within it. Is there anything in your zone that does not reflect the vibration you would like to access right here, right now? Some examples include unhealthy food, alcohol, drugs (legal or illegal), music (pay attention to the words), art (pay attention to what it is portraying), and so on. If so, get rid of it! That vibration no longer resonates with you. Replace the lower vibrational thing with a higher vibrational thing. The indicator of a higher vibration thing is one that makes you wholly and truly feel better or in some cases, even feel "high." Higher vibrational things may even make your entire being "vibrate" with joy. For example, the action of eating raw and whole foods, such as fruits, will most definitely allow you to feel a heightened state of ecstasy. **As you replace the lower vibrations that exist in your zone with higher vibrations, they will eventually begin to create a vibrational imprint onto your mind and cause the vibration you are operating at to increase, so your internal reality and external reality are in alignment with each other**. Once again, your zone has the biggest impact on you and has the power to shape you in any way you direct it to do so. You are the director of your zone. If you want to stop eating unhealthy foods, stop buying unhealthy foods and bringing them into your zone. If you want to stop smoking, do not allow smoking in your zone. If you want to stop drinking, do not allow alcohol into your zone. You get the idea. **Your zone is the closest physical reflection of you that exists, and therefore, your zone is sacred.** Treat it well. It is one of the most effective tools that can and will assist you in raising your vibration if you use it correctly.

Although you are in direct control of your zone, you can't always control what is going on in your external environment when you are in a public setting. What happens when you are not in your zone? What if you find yourself in a public setting in which you are surrounded by all of your vices that hurt your vibrational field? **When you are first going through your vibratory transformation, do your very best to stay out of situations that include things that exist on lower vibrations.** Most of the time, you have a choice. So long as these vices do not exist in your zone, which you indeed have control over, your mind will tune to the new vibration in which those vices no longer exist. Eventually, you will be able to be around all of your past vices without being bothered or seeing them as your vices anymore since they no longer exist at your vibration. In other words, you will no longer have a desire to indulge in the behaviors and actions you previously had trouble stopping. This is simply done by tuning out of resonance with them and into a new vibration in which they don't exist: a higher vibration. If you still call these poisons your "vices," you are only making it harder on yourself. **Begin by calling them your "lessons" instead of your "vices." Doing so will energetically imply that they exist not to hurt you and bring you down, but to teach you and lift you up.**

In regard to the second way of raising your vibration, people in your external environment are your greatest and most effective tools to do so. Being that everything is an energetic exchange, you must choose who you surround yourself with wisely. **Surrounding yourself with higher**

frequency beings will allow you to increase your vibration and, therefore, naturally and effortlessly grant you access to the ability to tune into your desired reality right here, right now. Additionally, surrounding yourself with higher frequency beings will naturally allow you to gain more access to a wider range of beneficial vibrations, which will naturally become a part of your field of energetic information. **Make a conscious effort to spend time with the people you admire in order to acquire the traits that they have through a productive and free flowing energetic exchange.** The following is a short entry I wrote in my journal on November 24th, 2019 about a new friend that has surfaced in my life. Someone that I have acquired great tools from through our energetic exchanges, just by being in his presence. The title of this entry is *"A Productive Energetic Exchange"*:

"These past 24 hours have taught me a lot about growth and humility. Barak has been the

angel sent into my life to attain such qualities. He is generally quiet and observant. He listens. When he does talk, EVERYONE listens. He chooses his words wisely and thinks before he speaks, a quality I truly admire and am now working on to access and incorporate into my life as I think it will be a beneficial quality to have for myself. I know the more time I spend with him; the more access I will naturally gain to the plane and frequency that he is vibrating at and therefore will experience the qualities I admire in him in my current reality. I have been and will continue to practice talking less and listening more, even when I have something to say. It brings me further and allows me to access a higher level of growth. Universe, thank you for blessing me with the opportunity to meet Barak and gain access to such wonderful tools. With infinite Love. Jason."

This entry is a direct reflection of how people in your external environment can be used as effective tools to raise your vibration. Being that everything is an energetic exchange, if you would like to access a certain reality, simply start by spending more time with people that are already vibrating in resonance with that reality. Doing so will allow you to gain the information they hold energetically and thus make your journey of vibratory transformation easier to access. If you want to be financially successful, simply start spending more time with others who are financially successful. If you want to be happy, simply start spending time with people who are happy. If you want to be healthy, simply start by spending time with people who are healthy. Doing so will allow you to expand your energetic field of information, thus giving you access to a wider range of innate tools and possibilities. **Surround yourself with people you admire, people you love, and people who add to your personal growth in life.**

When you do, your energetic exchange will be a productive one and even a medicinal one.

To assess if you will have a productive energetic exchange by spending time with someone, ask yourself the following questions:

1. **"Does this person have something in them that I would like to learn, adopt, and inherit as a tool, attribute, or characteristic of my own?"**

2. **"Can we both benefit and help each other energetically?"**

Asking yourself these questions will naturally filter the negative energy and unproductive relationships out of your life, whether it be a friendly relationship, a business relationship, a romantic relationship, and so on. Spending time with people who have the specific tools, attributes, and characteristics that you would like to attain in your current reality (out of admiration and not jealousy) will allow you to enter into an energetic exchange in which you will receive the information they hold. Doing so will allow you to tune into the vibration that resonates with these tools, attributes, and characteristics, and you will, therefore, be able to effortlessly adopt those tools, attributes, and characteristics into your own life.

If you ever find yourself in a situation where you are surrounded by people who produce an energetic exchange that does not consist of information you would like to carry in your field of energetic information, simply remove yourself from the situation. You have a choice, and the power is yours. Make the choice that serves you best and remember that it is never too late to do so. Your soul will be grateful for your decision. Always remember, if you want to stop indulging in certain actions or behaviors in your life, the key is not to resist those actions or behaviors, but to vibrationally rise above them. The first step to rising above the vibrations that those actions and behaviors exist at is by stopping to spend time with people who indulge in those actions and behaviors. In other words, if you want to stop smoking, stop spending time with people who smoke. If you want to stop drinking, stop spending time with people who drink. If you have seven friends who smoke, you will be the eighth. If you have nine friends who drink, you will be the tenth. **Ultimately, if you want to improve your habits by transmuting your negative habits into self-serving habits, change your surroundings! You are the only person who can do that. Change what is going on around you, and the change will be reflected within you.**

Every aspect of your external environment can be used as a tool to further improve the reflection your external reality imprints onto your mind. The things, actions, and behaviors you allow into your zone and the people you choose to spend your time with are just the tip of the iceberg. Being aware and in control of what you allow into your zone is a great way to shape and direct the vibration that your mind is operating at for your benefit. However, like any tool, if it is not used correctly, you can harm yourself. Observe and analyze your external reality to ensure that you are using it correctly to guide the vibration of your internal reality. Most importantly, stay alert and be conscious.

You now know the importance of the energetic exchange and how it may be used in order to gain tools, attributes, and characteristics from other souls that you look up to and admire. With this being said, you must be aware that there are certain actions that block the energetic exchange, while other actions ensure a successful energetic exchange between you and another soul. It is great to admire; however, there is a fine line between admiring and being jealous of what someone has, whether it is tangible or intangible. Admiration, gratitude, and unconditional forgiveness of others and yourself will allow the energetic exchange flow. On the other hand, comparison, which stems from fear and jealousy, is poisonous and will create resistance that will not allow for a successful and beneficial energetic exchange. **Comparison is the line that allows admiration and gratitude to evolve into fear and jealousy. Admiration, gratitude, and unconditional forgiveness flows; comparison blocks.**

Comparison: The Poisonous Pill

When you become stuck in the illusion of comparison, you no longer gain pleasure from having something; instead, you will gain pleasure only by having more than somebody else. Comparison is a poisonous pill that will surely block your ability to elevate and grow throughout your life. **Comparison is the poison that blocks the energetic exchange between you and**

any-body or any-thing since it creates resistance that does not allow for the energy to flow.

Ultimately, comparison is the killer of joy. The reason why comparison creates so much suffering is because it causes you to live in alignment with the illusion of separation and duality. Afterall, in order to compare yourself to something or somebody else, you must first understand that separation between you and somebody else is an illusion. **Energetically, separation is an impossibility.** In order to completely understand this, you must understand why separation and duality is an illusion in the first place. As Michael Jeffreys puts it, **"Separation is an illusion because ALL cannot be divided into separate parts. ALL contains everything; it leaves nothing out."** To better understand this, visualize a wavy ocean in your minds eye. The waves you see are simply the expression of energy moving through water; and therefore, although these waves may seem separate to the eye, they are not. **Waves are**

simply the infinite universal energy expressed in an infinitude of ways through the medium of water. Therefore, to poison one wave is to poison all waves. Well, we are no different. Each and every one of us are simply the same infinite universal energy expressed in an infinitude of different ways through the mediums that we call our body and soul. Although our physical bodies give us the illusion that we are separate from one another, we are all connected energetically, and we are, therefore, one infinite universal energy being expressed in an infinite amount of ways. **Once you dissolve the illusion of separation and see that we are all one universal energy being expressed in an infinite amount of ways, you will see, feel, and understand that my success is your success and your success is my success. The opposite is true as well. Your failure is my failure, and my failure is your failure. We are all one!** We live in one universe. There is no duality. That is why we call it a "uni-verse." **Oneness pervades all.** Every person, place, and experience are one. With that being said, every person, place, and experience are their own unique expression of this infinite universal energy. Duality and separation are merely illusions that create suffering when they are believed to be a truth. Living your life free of poisonous comparison and, therefore, free of fear and jealousy will allow you to greatly tap into the language of energy and benefit fully and wholly from the energetic exchanges that you constantly experience by allowing energy to flow with no resistance whatsoever.

Comparison is what allows for the duality of better and worse to exist. This duality creates suffering! Afterall, one can only exist when compared to the other. Only when we live in alignment with the illusion of separation and duality can comparison, and therefore fear and jealousy, be something we indulge in. **In order to live a life free of comparison, you must live a life through the lens**

of equanimity. One of my closest friends defined equanimity as the following:

"To not qualify a situation as good, bad, or anything in between. It is becoming present to the point where you see that everything just IS."

When living life through the lens of equanimity, comparison is non-existent, and your energetic exchanges will flow freely as there is no poison to create any resistance that will create a blockage in the flow of energy.

Once the illusion of separation and the truth of oneness is truly understood and experienced throughout your daily life, you will naturally and intuitively understand why to compare is so destructive to your own well-being. Being fearful or jealous of somebody and the tools they hold will no longer make sense to you, as you will see how thinking in such a way will only work against you. Remember, if fear or jealousy is a part of the equation, you will never be able to gain the tools, attributes, or characteristics that the other being holds since fear and jealousy inherently block the energetic exchange from occurring in the first place. There is absolutely no need to compare. Instead, practice equanimity, gratitude, and unconditional forgiveness as these are the keys and tools provided to you to ensure an unrestricted and free flow of energy in the world around you and the world within you. Using these keys and tools will allow you to access a life in which you have access to your limitless potential.

Gratitude: The Key to Happiness

Gratitude, simply defined, is the quality of being thankful and appreciative for all that IS. Expressing true gratitude is when you can willfully be grateful for everything in your life without labeling anything as good and bad or better and worse. This includes your past, present, and future hardships. Gratitude is the key that dissolves comparison. Therefore, gratitude is the key that dissolves the illusion of separation and duality. **Ultimately, gratitude is your key to pure and unconditional happiness.** It puts you in a state of flow with all that IS, without being stuck with the comparison of what could have been, should have been, or would have been. **Equanimity allows for you to understand that everything just IS; whereas, gratitude allows you to appreciate that everything just IS.** Practicing it will put you in a state of pure acceptance and appreciation of your life and everything in it, unconditionally. Expressing it is to naturally focus on what you do have instead of what you don't have. Expressing it is to focus on abundance instead of lack. Expressing it is to look at the glass half full instead of half empty. If you happen to be a person that sees the glass half empty, that is perfectly fine. You are not bound to that path of thought by any means, and just like you chose that path of thought, you can choose another path of thought, right here, right now. The choice is yours. Make the choice that serves you best and always remember to express your gratitude for being able to make such a choice in the first place. **Gratitude is what allows for your energetic exchanges to flow most freely.** Use it to help you through your journey of elevation throughout your life. It is a very effective tool in the language of energy to clear any energetic blockages and promote the free and unrestricted flow of energy in the world around you and the world within you. Although gratitude is an extremely important tool to use in order to enhance the flow of your energetic exchange, it will take you nowhere without applying the practice of unconditional forgiveness into your life. That is unconditional forgiveness of both yourself and of others.

Unconditional Forgiveness

Forgiveness, simply defined, is the act of letting go with no judgement whatsoever. The opposite of forgiveness is unforgiveness, and sometimes even revenge. Unconditional forgiveness promotes the free flow of energy; whereas, unforgiveness and revenge create energetic blockages. Remember, my joy is your joy, and your joy is my joy. This also means that my pain is your pain, and your pain is my pain. Although the pain may manifest differently, it exists on both ends. This is the balance of the universe: to inflict pain (whether physical or emotional) on another is to inflict pain on yourself. **Afterall, to poison one wave is to poison all waves.** Once this is understood, you will understand why unconditional forgiveness of yourself and others is so important. Living a life of unforgiveness and revenge is the equivalent of throwing a boulder into the middle of your own energetic path, thus restricting the free flow of energy. Forgiveness, on the other hand, instantaneously dissolves the boulder from your energetic path and re-instills the free flow of energy around you and within you. When you forgive, you significantly increase the flow of energy throughout your physical and emotional bodies and, therefore, increase the quality of your energetic exchanges.

Once you fully understand that we are all one and the separation of energy is an impossibility, you will see, feel, and understand that practicing unforgiveness and revenge will only harm you. **Emotions and actions, such as comparison, unforgiveness and revenge, restrict the flow of energy within you and, therefore, create energetic blockages within your system. These energetic blockages cause you to live a life of energetic "dis-ease," which always manifests into physical disease if not dissolved.** Afterall, physical disease is simply the reflection of an internal energetic blockage. This is a prime example of how your external reality is a direct reflection of your internal reality. Quite literally, physical disease or pain can only exist in your body where the flow of energy is being restricted. The practice of acupuncture is built on this very concept. In acupuncture, energy is referred to as *chi*. Acupuncture is the practice of placing tiny needles on specific meridian points, which is the map of your body that your *chi* flows through. The purpose of doing this is to dissolve any points where *chi* is being restricted and is causing an energetic blockage as a result. The purpose of the needles is to stimulate these meridians in order to re-instill and reconnect the free flow of *chi* (energy).

Unconditional forgiveness of both yourself and others is the ultimate key to unlocking the free and unrestricted flow of energy in the world around you and the world within you. Forgiving yourself is just as important as forgiving others, and you must do so unconditionally. Doing so will in fact act as a preventative health measure, as well as ensure a proper energetic flow throughout your body. Forgive unconditionally in order to give yourself the life you deserve, a life filled with unrestricted energetic exchanges and, therefore, a life in which you have limitless access to the infinite field of energetic information, as well as your highest potential.

You are now aware of the tools that have been provided to you in order to increase the flow of energy within you and around you. These tools (if used consciously) have the potential to increase the level of access you have to the energetic information you receive through any and every energetic exchange, whether it be with somebody or some thing. However, the energetic exchange works both ways. While you are receiving a large amount of energetic information at all times, you are also simultaneously emitting and, therefore, giving a large amount of energetic information at all times to every-being and every-thing around you. The energetic information you emit has a very powerful impact on your surroundings, which ultimately circles back to you since your surroundings have a very powerful impact on you. You must therefore emit your energetic information consciously for not only your benefit, but everyone else's benefit as well.

Surround Others Consciously

The beauty of balance in the universe allows you to not only use others as a tool to raise your vibration, but also to be that tool for others as well. You can use this tool to lift you up while simultaneously using this tool to lift up others, and, of course, by lifting up others, you in turn lift up yourself. **When the complete utility of this tool is realized, you will naturally want to stay away from emotions and actions, such as comparison, fear, jealousy, unforgiveness, and revenge, and attain a closer relationship with equanimity, gratitude, and unconditional forgiveness, as doing so will cause others to do the same.** This is simply due to the energetic fact that the people you spend the most time with will naturally be energetically imprinted by the vibration that you emit. That means that if you consciously exist on the vibration of sadness, eventually those you spend the most time with will begin to adopt the vibration of being that resonates with sadness. Alternatively, if you consciously exist on the vibration of happiness, eventually those you spend the most time with will begin to adopt the vibration of being that resonates with happiness! This in turn will benefit you since the people you spend the most time with are also the tools you use to raise your vibration.

Ever since a very young age, I've always promoted a healthy life style and lived accordingly. I was raised as a vegan. The books I read are generally health related, whether it be physical or emotional health. Due to my lifestyle, you can say that I emit a frequency that resonates with living a healthy life. The more I establish my vibration of health, the healthier others around me become. The vibration of health that I naturally emit due to my lifestyle is naturally received by others energetically. Beyond just receiving, I have seen that the more time I spend with those around me, the more they begin to adopt this vibration into their own lives, and their physical actions reflect it. Suddenly, they start eating healthier; they decide they don't want to drink anymore, and smoking becomes a past-time. It's quite beautiful actually! What is even more beautiful is that just being in the presence of others is enough to create such a shift. Thanks to the energetic exchange that is constantly occurring between every being and every thing, just being in the presence of others imprints the vibration of health onto them, and they naturally begin resonating with that reality. This is the energetic exchange in action, and this is how it can be beautifully used as a tool to benefit others around you and, therefore, benefit yourself. Not only do high vibrational beings attract other high vibrational beings, but high vibrational beings can also help low vibrational beings transform.

Remember, just like the vibration of the people in your environment affect your vibration of being, so does your vibration affect the vibration of being of the people in your environment. You are simply a vibrating vessel that is constantly giving and receiving energy from every being and every thing. What you emit is what others will receive. For this reason, you must speak consciously, think consciously, and act consciously, as all of these components translate to energetic information that is being transferred to others around you just by your being in their presence. When you begin to speak consciously, think consciously, and act consciously, not only will you be able to elevate your own vibration, but your own elevated vibration will be imprinted onto others around you, in turn helping them raise their vibration of being just by being in your presence. The elevated vibration of those around you will then create an external environment that directly reflects the vibration that you are consciously choosing to experience through speech, thought, and action, which will continue feeding your cycle of personal growth and elevation. It is important to remember that everything is an energetic exchange, so you must speak, think, and act consciously when you surround yourself with others to ensure both ends of the exchange are beneficial. **If you want to change your surroundings and help others around you, simply reflect that which you want to see in others in yourself.** Once you do, spending time with others will be all you must do in order to help them transform. Always remember, by helping others, you are helping yourself. For this reason, always remember to make an effort to surround others consciously.

The Power of Touch

Although just being in something's or somebody's presence is enough to facilitate an energetic exchange, *touch* **can and will most definitely enhance the energetic information you are able to access from the exchange.** This is why eating food with your hands and walking barefoot causes such a powerful exchange of energetic information. Physical touch is a powerful and direct way to exchange energetic information. With this being so, you must be conscious of who and what you touch, as well as who and what you let touch you. Since touch greatly enhances the energetic exchange, make sure you are only touching and being touched by those with whom you would like to exchange energetic information with.

Energetic Cleansing

Being that everything is an energetic exchange, you may find yourself in situations where you have inherited energetic information from somebody or something around you that has the potential to harm you. For example, if you are ever in a situation where you feel somebody is subliminally and energetically conveying jealousy or fear towards you, it is important to cleanse yourself in order to release these energetic poisons from your system. If you ever feel that you have entered an energetic exchange that has the potential to harm you energetically, whether through touch or any other medium, washing yourself with water is one of the greatest tools to cleanse yourself of this energy, specifically ocean water. Burning incense, specifically sage, also facilitates your energetic cleansing process since it transforms resistant negative energy into flowing positive energy.

CHAPTER 4

APPRECIATING CHANGE

"Fearing change is fearing growth.
The faster you are able to change, the faster
you are able to grow."

With all of these new internal and external tools that you have gained to reach your highest potential in this present moment there will come an inevitable change. A change of behavior. A change of action. A change of thought. A change of friends. A change of lifestyle. The most important thing to remember is that **you have no obligation to be the same person you were one year ago, one month ago, one week ago, one day ago, one hour ago, one minute ago, or even one second ago. Many of us fear change for many reasons, such as the fear of instability as you go through this period of change and transformation. This fear is also referred to as the fear of the unknown.** This is the fear of not knowing what such a change will result in. This fear of instability and uncertainty has led many people to resist change in order to avoid experiencing the fear in the first place. Many of us have become comfortable with being uncomfortable because at least we know what that un-comfortability consists of. Once again, this all stems from fearing the unknown. The unknown, in this case of change, is what your life will be like after claiming your power back with the tools you have been shown and provided with. **Resisting change is contractive. Accepting change is expansive.** It is time to let go of the fear of change and dissolve that growth stunting poison out of our system once and for all. In order to do so, you must first understand why the fear exists.

Understanding the Fear

I want you to envision your life as a tall tower made of blocks. Your foundation, that which is holding up your tower, is also made of blocks, and we all know that every tower must have a strong foundation in order to stand tall and strong. Your foundation in this case represents your words, your thoughts, your beliefs, and of course your environment and surroundings. There comes a point in life when you realize a block in your foundation no longer serves your tower and it must be replaced with a stronger foundational block. To change this foundational block, you are going to have to remove it in order to replace it with a new foundation block that is stronger and will, therefore, allow for you to build a taller and more stable tower. The reason why we experience fear of change is not because we have to remove one block in order to replace it with another. **The reason why we experience fear of change is due to that period of time in between removing the old foundational block and replacing it with a stronger foundation block when there is no block in your foundation at all.** This is when your whole tower feels unstable and wobbly. We fear this period of time because we are unfamiliar with it, and the concept of unknowingness during this period of time is the underlying theme of the experience, which can make you feel unjustifiably vulnerable.

Overcoming the Fear

In order to overcome the fear of change, you must deal directly with understanding and appreciating that period of instability and unknowingness. In order to be appreciative of instability and unknowingness, you must understand that without them, growth would never be able to exist in your life. You must understand that it is because of that period of instability and unknowingness that you can experience an eternal lifetime of elevation and growth. That short period of instability and unknowingness is the reason why you can make your tower taller. From here on out, lose the fear of change. There is no longer a need to fear! Don't fear that period of instability and unknowingness. Instead, appreciate it. Be grateful for it. Embrace it because it is the only thing that gives you the ability to transform and learn more about life, as well as yourself. It's the only reason you are able to strengthen your foundation and build a taller tower. Now that you understand how important and necessary this period of instability and unknowingness is, instead of running away from it, run towards it! Afterall, it exists to serve you in your life.

The Transformation

Once you completely embrace change and allow it to be a part of your life, you will experience what I like the call "the transformation phase." The transformation phase is what you used to be afraid of, but you have now learned to appreciate and be grateful for as is it is a direct portal to both internal and external personal growth and transformation. For the sake of understanding how to deal with the transformation phase, consider the following scenario:

For years, you have been very close with who you call your best friend. You speak every day and you spend a lot of time together. One day you realize that this best friend of yours no longer resonates with the vibration that you would like to experience life through. In others words, the behaviors and actions your friend expresses are not a reflection of the reality you would like to access in the present moment. You try to keep the friendship going, but with time, you realize that you are growing apart, and keeping this friend as a close person in your life will only stunt your growth. So, you make a bold decision, and you decide to respectfully keep your distance and keep this friend out of your "zone" as this friend no longer reflects the vibration you would like to resonate with.

The moment you made the decision to keep your distance to energetically serve your personal growth is the moment you entered the transformational phase. The hours that you used to spend speaking every day and hanging out every night now have the ability to be filled with people and actions that do reflect the new vibration that you would like to resonate with, only this will not happen over night. As you start learning how to spend your new free time in ways that reflect a higher vibration of being, your vibration of being will begin to transform and so will your life. As your vibration rises, other beings vibrating in resonance with you will be energetically attracted to you. **Afterall, your vibe attracts your tribe.** The transformation phase is a beautiful time period in the process of change. Be conscious of your vibration when you are experiencing it. **The vibration you transform into during the transformation phase will dictate the reality that you are going to access next.**

Letting Go

Letting go is a must in the transformation phase. Without it, no transformation would be able to take place. Many of us see letting go as a negative or sad part of life. It's time to change that perception and dissolve the fear of letting go. Whether it be a relationship, the passing of a loved one, or a friendship that no longer serves you, letting go can only result in one outcome. **The process of letting go gives space for new experiences and relationships to manifest in your life.** So, I urge you to take the next few minutes to self-reflect. See what actions, beliefs, relationships, or thoughts no longer serve you (no longer exist at the vibration you would like to resonate with), and LET GO! Embrace the change. Let the old vibration fade away and watch the new vibration appear.

CHAPTER 5

LESS DOING, MORE BEING

"Doing is a function of the body. Being is a function of the soul"

Visualize a lake in your mind's eye. This lake is one thousand feet deep. On the surface of the lake you may have sunny days, cloudy days, rainy days, stormy days, calm days, wavy days, and so on. However, no matter what is occurring on the surface of the lake, when you dive deep down into that lake, the water will always be still. Even if a hurricane is happening on the surface, it makes no difference. At one thousand feet deep, there will always be stillness. **The lake is a representation of you. The surface of the lake where the water is always changing represents your state of doing, and the depths of the lake where the water is always still represents your state of being**. Doing is a function of the body, whereas being is a function of the soul. Your body resides in the state of doing, and your soul resides in the state of being. Ultimately, your being state is where your stillness and inner peace reside.

Do Less, Be More

———

Nowadays, the average person does not wake up excited to go to work. They simply go to work because it is necessary in order to survive. Although the necessity exists, this mindset has led humanity down a sick path of sadness—a path that is primarily focused on *doing* instead of *being*. This path has led us to a place that causes one to not BE happy at work (which, for most, takes up a major part of their day) if they don't like what they DO for a living. The reason you see people that materialistically have everything in the world, yet are still unsatisfied and sad in life, is because they are trying to gain happiness through their state of doing, instead of their state of being. This is only a temporary solution, because next time a storm comes, their state of doing will be affected while their state of being will remain untouched by even the wildest and most chaotic storms. **No matter what you are doing, whether you like it or not is irrelevant. Unconditional happiness is not**

contingent on your state of doing but on your state of being.

When you focus on being instead of doing, what you are doing becomes irrelevant. Whether you are a janitor or the CEO of a fortune 500 company, what you do is not what counts. It's what you are being when you do whatever it is that you do that makes all the difference! This is what creates true bliss and internal unconditional joy and happiness. Next time an external circumstance comes your way that makes you feel upset, sad, or depressed, dive deep within yourself where your stillness resides and reclaim your state of being. Feel that stillness and inner peace that nobody can take away from you, the inner stillness and inner peace that no external circumstance has the power to affect. **When you live through a state of being instead of a state of doing, nobody and no thing can hurt you anymore. You become invincible, which is the energetic truth of who you are.** Remember, true bliss has nothing to do with your external circumstances. **True bliss is when your internal reality is not contingent on your external reality.** Live in your being state. Afterall, your soul doesn't care what you do for a living, and when you are no longer in your present form, neither will you. Your soul only cares about what you are being while you do whatever it is that you do. So, no matter what you are doing, make sure to always BE. Be grateful. Be present. Be you!

Being Yourself

So many of us live a life through the lens of needing validation and approval from others in order to feel accepted. This path of thought causes us to put on a mask that consist of things we "should" be like and "should" have instead of just being our true and whole selves with no supplementation. We live in a constant state of fear of what others think about us and how they see us. As a result, we disconnect from ourselves in order to adapt and to feel accepted. We feel the need to follow the fashion trends and buy the newest phone or computer the moment it comes out just because everyone else does, even if we don't wholeheartedly like it. Eventually, this disconnection leads us to a place where we forget who we are and live in a constant place of fear since our feeling of acceptance is based on what we are doing instead of who are we being. We constantly look externally for acceptance instead of internally, but we've got it all backwards. **In order to be accepted by others, you must first accept yourself.** It has nothing to do with the job you have, the shoes you wear, or the home you live in. There is no longer a need to adapt because what you are doing is no longer relevant. It's who you are being that matters. So, be yourself!

Water: The Element that IS

Water is not the essence of life, energy is. However, water does hold a massive amount of energetic information that has the potential to teach us a life worth of lessons, if not more.

On December 27th 2019, I wrote the following entry in my journal:

"Water… it's beauty is beyond what words can express. We have so much to learn from this beautiful element. It is my favorite medium to watch energy flow through. It teaches us purity, adaptability, balance, and absolute permanence of all that IS, otherwise known as "being". Just look at water during a storm. High winds come and create waves, making the water chaotic. After some time, the storm passes, the winds calm down, and so does the water. What happened in this scenario is that the water allowed for the chaotic energy to flow through it and create what we call waves. However, eventually when that chaotic energy completes its cycle of flowing through the water,

*the water always returns right back to its pure
state of stillness and wavelessness."*

Water allows energy to flow through it with no judgement, no resistance. No matter how powerful the storm may be, it always returns back to stillness. Applying the qualities that water teaches us to our own lives allows for life to flow seamlessly. Just like water, we should take the path of least resistance while learning and acknowledging every lesson along the way with pure acceptance. In other words, we should acknowledge and learn from what it is that we are doing or what it is that is being done to us while always remaining in a pure state of being. **Ultimately, water teaches us how to let our state of doing pass right through us with no resistance or judgement while still acknowledging and learning from it in order to be in touch with our stillness that exists internally, in the pure state of being.**

CHAPTER 6

YOUR BODY IS YOUR SANCTUARY

"Physical sickness handicaps your soul, whereas physical health benefits your soul."

n order to apply and tap into the language of energy holistically, you must attain a high level of awareness. In order to attain a high level of awareness, you must be spiritually healthy. In order to be spiritually healthy, you must be physically healthy. In other words, it all starts with your body! **Your body is the sanctuary that houses your spirit and soul. Physical sickness handicaps spiritual capability, whereas physical health ensures and promotes spiritual capability.** Ultimately, your body must be healthy and energetically aligned in order to be able to attain a higher level of awareness. As you reach a higher level of awareness, you will be able to effortlessly apply the language of energy into your life. This means that you will be able to gain access to any and every reality in the present moment; you will be able to choose your words wisely in an effortless manner; you will be able to facilitate, direct, and be aware of the energetic exchange; you will embrace and appreciate change in your life; and you will live in a pure state of being.

You will also be able to expand on the language of energy in your own unique and creative way.

You Are What You Eat

The food that we consume can be used as a great tool to raise our vibration and, therefore, our level of awareness. However, most of us unknowingly eat in such a way that lowers our vibration and awareness, and thus, the result is handicapping up both physically and spiritually. You can have the best car in the world, but if you don't provide it with the right fuel, it won't run properly. Your body is no different. The food you consume is the fuel that your body operates on which is why it is so important. **Food is simply energy expressed in physical and edible form.** In other words, **each food holds its own vibration. What you consume is in turn the vibration that you adopt, inherit, and therefore become. You are what you eat!** Many of us want to access a high level of awareness while eating foods that do not reflect the vibration of high awareness. **You cannot eat low vibrational food and expect to vibrate high, just as you cannot eat dead food and expect to live.**

Due to the obsolescence of the energetic connection between us and our food in our daily lives, we have allowed ourselves to eat poisons, such as gluten, dairy, dead flesh, and processed foods. Also due to the obsolescence of the energetic connection between us and our food in our daily lives, we don't understand why these poisons are poisons to begin with. We are so disconnected that we even dare to call them *food* in the first place. There are many misconceptions about food in the modern world, and these misconceptions arise from the fact that we no longer experience a direct energetic exchange between us and the food that we eat. If we did, anything that consisted of gluten, dairy, or dead flesh, let alone anything processed, would make you sick before it even entered your body.

Just think about it logically. With the exception of domesticated animals, are there any other animals on this planet that eat food that has been processed? No. So why do we? Is there any other animal on this planet that drinks milk from a different species of animal, let alone drinks milk past its own mother's maturation of breast feeding? No, so why do we? Is there any other animal on this planet that needs to cook its dead flesh, let alone its food, before consuming it? No, so why do we? The only reason we cook dead flesh in the first place is because we would get sick if we ate it raw. Logically, doesn't that mean we shouldn't be consuming it in the first place? We take part in all of these absurdities and see nothing wrong with them due to our energetic disconnect between us and the natural world. This disconnect has led us to live a life of decreased physical health and, therefore, experience life through a lower state of awareness, which is a spiritual handicap.

High vibrational food is food you don't have to process, let alone cook, in order to eat. High vibrational food is food that gets its energy from the highest source of energy, the sun. That leaves us with real food: fruits, most vegetables, herbs, and nuts. It is important to note that not all vegetables and herbs are to be used as food. For example, onion and garlic are not meant to be used as food, rather they are to be used as medicine. In order to be physically healthy, reconnecting to true and high vibrational food is the first step that must be taken. **As you eat cleaner, you will vibrate higher. As you vibrate higher, you will become more aware. As you become more aware, you will be able to tap into the infinite language of energy and effortlessly apply its beauty into your daily life.** Just look at the way the world is currently transforming. We are experiencing a mass shift in consciousness and spiritual awareness. A big part of this shift is a change in the food that we collectively consume.

The world is slowly but surely shifting towards a plant-based lifestyle. That is because the vibration of plant-based and raw food, such as uncooked fruits and vegetables, is in vibrational alignment with a higher vibrational frequency, and, therefore, a higher state of awareness. I highly recommend reading *Life Changing Foods* by Anthony Williams to gain more in-depth guidance on what to eat to live a life of heightened awareness. The book covers both the physical health benefits, as well as the energetic information that each food gives you through the energetic exchange.

Toxins Cause "Dis-ease"

Toxins have become a major part of our daily lives. There are hormones in the food we consume. There is chlorine and fluoride in the water we drink. There are pollutants in the air that we breathe. We have become so energetically disconnected that we no longer feel their immediate impact and, therefore, wake up one day with a life-threatening disease not understanding where it came from. The fact is, the disease didn't begin the day you were diagnosed, but way before that time. **What is now a physical disease first started as energetic "dis-ease," which eventually manifests to physical "dis-ease," otherwise known as** *disease***.**

There are two types of toxins in the world: voluntary toxins and involuntary toxins. The involuntary toxins are the ones you can't always control based on your environment, such as what is unknowingly in the food you eat, the water you drink, and the air you breathe. Voluntary toxins, on the other hand, are toxins that we have direct control over, such as low vibrational foods, alcohol, and the inhalation of smoke, to name a few. These voluntary toxins lower your vibration and, therefore, lower your level of awareness. This in turn leads to a handicapped ability to tap into the infinite language of energy. Before you eat that junk food, smoke that cigarette, or drink that tequila, ask yourself the following question:

Do I want to live in a dirty home?

Your body is the most intimate home that you have, and the cleaner it is, the more you can achieve both physically and spiritually. Keep reminding yourself of this question repeatedly. It will assist you in effortlessly living a cleaner life, free of toxicity. Keep your body clean. Your soul deserves it.

The Root: Emotional Toxicity

The root of all physical voluntary toxicity we allow into our bodies begins with emotional toxicity. Afterall, being that your external reality is a direct reflection of your internal reality, the external voluntary toxicity you willingly allow to enter into your body is a direct reflection of the internal emotional toxicity that exists within your body. Some toxic emotions include judgement, conditional love, comparison, jealousy, fear, unforgiveness, and revenge, to name a few. All of these emotions restrict the flow of energy, which is ultimately the root of all physical disease. Restricting the flow of energy through toxic emotions will set you on a path filled with sickness and disease since the energetic blockage will cause you to be vibrationally numb. This numbness will not allow you to feel the immediate toxic impact of the physical voluntary toxins you allow to enter into your body, such as poisonous food, alcohol, and the inhalation of smoke. This, too, will result in the adoption of a lower vibrational state of being, which will ultimately lower your level of awareness and create yet another spiritual handicap for yourself. Indulging in the practice of allowing toxic emotions into your life will ultimately restrict the flow of energy around you and within you, which will make you physically sick and will, therefore, make you unable to tap into the infinite language of energy and effortlessly apply its beauty into your life.

Reconnecting to Energetic Flow and Alignment

The universe along with everything it is made up of is always striving for energetic balance and energetic flow. Due to our energetic disconnect, we have created things like the pharmaceutical drug industry, which is a direct reflection of the absurd belief that we are smarter than our bodies. **We have lost touch with the infinite energetic intelligence of the universe that flows through us eternally. This intelligence is self-balancing and self-healing. The belief that we need to interfere in order to heal is an absurdity that simply stems out of our energetic disconnect with the natural world.** This universal intelligence that flows through us infinitely is beyond what the mind can comprehend and has more power to heal than any medicine ever developed by a human being. **The only thing we have to do is not get in its way.** This is why fasting, specifically water fasting, is so powerful!

Fasting has the power and ability to reconnect us energetically, which in turn causes us to re-balance and heal any energetic blockages that may exist within our physical or emotional bodies. Fasting allows for the body to do what it always strives to do: reclaim energetic balance and energetic flow. The way it works energetically is actually quite simple. Every time we consume food, and this includes whole and healthy foods as well, our body needs to allocate energy to digest that food. The fact that it needs to allocate energy for digestion means it is compromising on the allocation of energy for healing purposes. Just look at the natural world. **When an animal experiences any form of sickness, it intuitively stops eating in order to re-allocate and refocus its energy from digesting its food to healing its body. Fasting is simply the action of not getting in the way of your body's healing process.** It allows for your body to allocate its energy to heal on both the physical and emotional level.

As your body heals, you will experience both a physical and an emotional detox. This detox is simply the removal of lower vibrations (in the forms of physical toxins and emotional toxins) from your body in order to transform to a higher vibration and, therefore, to a higher level of awareness. On the physical level, you may get acne, have bad breath, emit intense body odor, and so on. Everybody detoxes differently. On the emotional level, you will experience a diversity of emotional releases. This may cause temporary anxiety, nervousness, or even depression. You may feel inclined to scream, cry, get angry, laugh, and so on. Again, everybody detoxes differently. It is important to remember that **emotional detox always induces a physical detox.** This is why when you cry (the expression of an emotional release), you get a runny nose (physical release). Going through this detox period is extremely important. It is what allows for an unrestricted flow of energy to be re-established, which in turn will allow you to live a life clear of any energetic blockages, so you can attain a higher level of awareness and, therefore, tap into the infinite language of energy and effortlessly apply its beauty into your life! Now that you understand the power of fasting, don't be afraid of it. Your body is an incredible tool that can bring you to very high places, all you have to do is not get in its way.

The Language of Energy in Action

By now, it is probably most apparent to you that most of us live lives led by energetic disconnection. The ways in which we act with ourselves and one another, both physically and emotionally, as well as the food that we consume, are direct reflections of this energetic disconnection. Because of it, we have forgotten the infinite power and strength that is within us. Because of it, we have lost touch with the natural world, and, therefore, we have lost touch with understanding and feeling the language of energy. Most importantly, **we have lost touch with ourselves.**

Hopefully by now, you have gained a better understanding of the principles, which make up this beautiful language of energy that interconnects all beings and all things of the universe. You have been given the tools to reconnect to this universal language in turn granting you access to the formless, where all possibilities exist. **The more you connect to the principles of this beautiful language and allow this universal and intelligent energy to flow through you with no resistance, the more you will be able to intuitively feel and understand the energetic universe in which you live in.** In doing so, you will be able to reclaim the power and direction you have to direct this energy in a way that fits you best. **You will know that you are worthy when you don't choose the road of least resistance to make your life easy but when you choose the road of the most growth, which is**

generally the bumpiest, and turn it into the road of least resistance through your state of being and unconditional understanding and love for all that IS, just as water does.

On February 28th, 2020, I wrote the following entry in my journal:

"Today is February 28th, 2020. I have officially completed The Language of Energy, a book I began writing exactly two weeks ago. The book is finished from front cover to back cover. I am sitting here, smiling, yet not surprised. I'm not surprised because I did exactly what I wrote about in order to manifest any reality, right here, right now. I set my intent aligned with the

I-AM formula, I believed undoubtedly, and I visualized it all very clearly. I made sure to choose my words wisely and speak consciously when it came to anything about the book, I allowed for the energetic exchange between my current reality and the reality in which this book existed to flow freely with no blockages whatsoever, I acknowledged and accepted the fact that I was going to have to change my daily routine and sleep a little less for a period of time in order to give room for this book to fit into my new reality, I made sure to "be" the book instead of "do" the book, and lastly, I made sure to feed my body high vibrational foods to ensure the high vibrational flow of energy throughout the process. Two weeks later, I am sitting here writing a journal entry that reflects the success of accessing that reality which I envisioned just fourteen days ago in my present moment. This is the power of applying the language of energy in action and it is absolutely beautiful! Although I physically wrote this book, energetically I did not write anything. This book is merely an expression of the infinite source of energy that flows through every-being and every-thing. This book was not written by me, but through me. This idea applies to every writer, singer, dancer, and any other form of creator. This idea is quite humbling because it allows one to understand that they never actually create anything, because everything already exists. We are simply being used as a tool by the universe to express its infinite, eternal, and ever-present flow of energy. Thank you, Universe, for blessing me with the ability to perceive the energetic universe so effortlessly and most importantly, thank you for granting me the ability to formulate and structure it all in such a way that I can share it with the rest of the world. Thank you for so elegantly flowing through me. With infinite Love, Jason."

What occurs in your life from here on out you will see not as a matter of luck, but a matter of choice. You are the director. Practice applying the principles of this omni-present universal language into your daily life. Experiment with it. See where it takes you. **Remember, my intention is not to influence you, rather it is to teach you how not to be influenced.** Experiment with the tools and gifts you have been granted and expand on the infinite language of energy in your own and unique way. Practice accessing instead of creating; choose your words wisely by being conscious and in the present moment; facilitate and become more aware of the energetic exchange that occurs between all beings and all things; appreciate change as it will only result in growth; start focusing on being instead of doing; and treat your body as the sanctuary that it is to increase your level of awareness and further connect to the energetic universe around you and within you.

Remember, we are all simply the expression of the infinite and ever-present source of universal energy. We are all this energy and, therefore, nothing separates us. We are all ONE. We are here to help one another elevate throughout our

individual paths of life, so we can all collectively reach our destiny as one infinite formless expression of Light, so we can eventually touch the Light. Now that you have been granted the tools and gifts that exist within the language of energy, use them to spread your knowledge, spread your wisdom, and spread your Light. We are all souls, getting closer and closer to our collective destiny; a time of absolute unity, and unconditional Love.

I wish you all a journey filled with Light, Peace, and Love

—Jason

Printed in Great Britain
by Amazon